YELLOW
CRANE

YELLOW

SUSAN

POEMS

CRANE

GILLIS

BRICK BOOKS

LIBRARY AND ARCHIVES CANADA CATALOGUING IN PUBLICATION

Gillis, Susan, author
Yellow crane / Susan Gillis.
Poems.
Issued in print and electronic formats.
ISBN 978-1-77131-491-6 (softcover).
ISBN 978-1-77131-493-0 (pdf).
ISBN 978-1-77131-492-3 (epub)
I. Title.
ps8563.i5125y45 2018   c811'.54   c2018-902175-6   c2018-902176-4

We acknowledge the Canada Council for the Arts, the Government of Canada through the Canada Book Fund, and the Ontario Arts Council for their support of our publishing program.

 Canada Council   Conseil des Arts
for the Arts   du Canada

 Canadian   Patrimoine
Heritage   canadien

 ONTARIO ARTS COUNCIL
CONSEIL DES ARTS DE L'ONTARIO
an Ontario government agency
un organisme du gouvernement de l'Ontario

The author photo was taken by John Steffler.
The book is set in Mercury and Ideal Sans by Hoefler & Co.
The cover image is by agaz / photocase.com.
Design and layout by Natalie Olsen, Kisscut Design.
Printed and bound by Coach House Printing.

BRICK BOOKS
431 Boler Road, Box 20081
London, Ontario N6K 4G6
www.brickbooks.ca

CONTENTS

How far off are those years, mine and not mine,

When one wrote poems on Italy

Telling about evenings in the fields of Siena

Or about cicadas in Sicilian ruins.

— **Czesław Miłosz**

OVERTURE

For awhile as children we didn't know time existed.

Then time teased us; eager to catch up with it, we wanted to have sex with stars, or just anyone, to drive, to drink, to travel; we wanted to be old enough.

Eventually we were, but still time was ahead of us. Now we wanted to be old enough to speak our minds without fear of consequence, to do things we weren't ready for just yet but someday; we got together with time and made plans.

Only that day never came. Instead, we woke from a dream of being chased and realized we'd switched ends; now time was taunting us to come back.

Our children grew up too fast, or had never materialized at all; we couldn't believe we'd been so good looking, in spite of our ridiculous outfits and the hair.

For a long while a battle raged. Cunning, trickery, deceit, excellence, lists — we used them all.

Gradually we became tired of our heroics. We saw where this was going, and began to befriend time.

Soon Arthurian England didn't seem so different; we could imagine the sound of crickets in the Roman Coliseum. Uruk could be a living place, with friends and romance and intrigue and all the other elements of the mysteries we'd taken up reading.

Deep time seemed like a place we might visit, like the Danube or Antarctica.

We collected brochures, planned our next move, the next-to-last or next-to-next-to-last, hand in hand with time, who seemed at last to be giving us good advice.

We got ready.

Took us a while, didn't it?

OBELISK

1

Light and shadow sweep the field, hasty, hurried.

The wind that pushes the clouds that make the shadows is high.

The hay is not waving, only the light on the hay.

And then the wind spirals down, down, the hay in whorls, shaking.

A shadow crosses.

On my left the stone wall springs to light, flowering plants in the niches, radiant.

This is how we don't write anymore: stone walls, hayfields, ruins, the beauty of ruins.

Charged with being *too politicized*, Czesław Miłosz answers that he *can* write the senses, *would like to, therefore* doesn't.

If you have a nail in your shoe, what then? Do you love that nail?

No, or yes, it's the same thing.

I stretch out my legs and stare over the field.

Pine, pine, spruce, fir, pine.

Wind in the poplars over Willow Pond.

Yes, I would like to be a poet of the world.

New weather drifting toward me over the hay.

---

1 Czesław Miłosz's "In Milan" is a poem I keep going back to for its many conundrums, not least of which is whether he loves the nail. 2 John Dixon Hunt's collection of essays, *Gardens and the Picturesque*, opens with a useful introduction on the cultural landscape. It's impossible to be alive

Daffodils and bluebells have naturalized in the grass between the driveway and Woodshed Hill.

When I pick them and bunch them in a jar I'm just doing what comes naturally, a thing that's second nature, a choice that's ceased to be a choice.

A whole-heartedly embraced preference, like swimming or lying in the hammock. It's warm enough now to lie in the hammock between the shed and the tree at the edge of the rock pile, and read.

John Dixon Hunt tells me that *Cicero termed what we would call the cultural landscape a second nature.*

'Alteram naturam,' a landscape of bridges, roads, harbours, fields — in short, all of the elements which men and women introduce into the physical world to make it more habitable, to make it serve their purposes.

A stone placed on end in a pile of stones in a clearing.

I'm glad Hunt recognizes more than one gender in the cultural landscape. Then grammar forces him aside, as though he's not there.

Hunt continues, ignoring me. *Cicero's phrase 'a second nature' of course implies a first; though he does not specify this, we may take it that he implies a primal nature, an unmediated world before humans invaded, altered, and augmented it, a world without any roads, ports, paths, terraces, vineyards, etc. Today we might call it the wilderness.*

Don McKay enters with a playful grin. *Well, naturally. Place is just wilderness to which history has happened.*

Walter Benjamin, who has stopped in briefly, chops the air with his hand. *This is exactly how one pictures the angel of history!*

Swaying gently, the hammock brushes an obelisk that has appeared beside it in the clearing.

---

and not have some kind of imprint on the world. At Castle Howard, edifices — obelisk, pyramid, temple, gate, and more — stake their claims over the land with allusions to the classical world. In the same way, its fields and copses provide grazing pastures and hunting grounds, double

3

On every continent, in every city, on waysides, in fields, in underground bunkers, everywhere bones are left to decompose, pieces of metal to explode, wreckage piled upon wreckage —

Everywhere we can't explain human cruelty, call it animal, call it monster, shaking our heads —

Everywhere *what we hold to as our own* is enshrined in steel and stone, or stretched on hooks between a tree and the corner-post of a shed, inviting us to lie down in good weather —

---

as wildlife habitats, and open up pleasing, sometimes breathtaking, vistas. "Better" even than beautiful paintings, these were designed to be scenes people could actually enter. Are the fields and copses more than fields and copses, then, or less? **3** Every time I read it, Walter Benjamin's

4

The history of civilization! Pomp, medals, monuments. *Sartorial splendours*. The achievements of the victors.

Why not *a history centred on the sufferings of the vanquished?*

Seriously, why?

---

famous passage in *Theses on the Philosophy of History* on Paul Klee's paint-ing *Angelus Novus* sends shivers through me. Many have borrowed from it; Carolyn Forché found a title and more there for her book *The Angel of History*. And I always misremember Wim Wender's film *Wings of Desire*

A partial list of libraries and archives destroyed by human action:

Xianyang Palace and State Archive, destroyed 206 BCE
Libraries of Alexandria, date of destruction disputed
Nalanda University, destroyed 1193
Imperial Library of Constantinople, destroyed 1204
Maya Codices of the Yucatan, destroyed 1562
Library of Congress, Washington, destroyed 1814
National Library of Serbia, destroyed 1941
The Libraries of Fisheries and Oceans Canada, destroyed 2013

In the name of what, exactly?

---

quoting from this passage. (It doesn't. Although that film has a great many instances of beautiful language, this passage isn't among them.)
4 Virginia Woolf links "sartorial splendours" with "ruined houses, dead bodies" in her essay *Three Guineas*. I've carried this idea around for

Deep in the Retirement of that Wood, the God of Sleep has reared his Habitation.

And giants sleep among us there, and there among us monsters grow.

The smell of tea rises together with the clatter of a passing truck.

---

decades. It comes back to me when I read Stuart Jeffries on Benjamin's *The Arcades Project* in the *Guardian*.   **5** On the destruction of the libraries of Fisheries and Oceans Canada by the government of Canada under Stephen Harper, *The Tyee* reports: "Scientists who use the libraries say

I am for … I could compose right now … No one can accuse me … I do not deny … Yes, I would like … That's why I don't allow myself …

Miłosz, walking on the Piazza del Duomo in Milan. It's late. The friends have probably been drinking.

Thought, says Miłosz, *has less weight than the word* lemon.

Thought, *lemon*. Thought, *lemon*. I weigh them in my hands.

Whatever it is I want to do, it can't be done without suffering, which naturally I want to avoid, so I avoid doing the thing I desire.

Not Miłosz.

Miłosz isn't avoiding anything.

---

priceless information, essential for the legal and political security of Canada's waterways as well as the defence of the longest coastline in the world, was thrown into dustbins, burned or scavenged by private consultants. In Winnipeg, a consultant's group operating for Manitoba

Sikong Tu's twenty-four styles of poetry:

1, Potent, Undifferentiated
2, Limpid and Calm
3, Delicate-Fresh and Rich-Lush
4, Firm and Self-Possessed
5, Lofty and Ancient
6, Decorous and Dignified

and so on ...

Hydro backed up a truck to collect materials from the dismantled library."
6 Architects in the garden, as William Gilpin's fictional "Dialogue" between two gentlemen on the newly-designed gardens at Stowe in 1748 elaborates, concern themselves with (among other things) the

9

Donald Revell flies, he says, every week from his home in one state to his teaching job in another. He's dismayed when the people he sits next to say they want to build golf courses on the wilderness land they're flying over.

Write, he says, *carelessly,* write the obvious, write trusting the world to make content, to make meaning, put aside mind and thought.

Xi Chuan says style comes if you write honestly about your times.

The buds of style hide themselves in human sufferings, weaknesses, the brightness and darkness of the nature, the shadows of philosophy, social changes.

On Sikong Tu's "Twenty-Four Gradings of Poems": *It's really difficult to be a poet! You have to develop such sensitive ears that you are able to catch the slightest sound made by a needle falling down to the ground.*

Xi Chuan says that Sikong Tu *is absolutely correct, but maybe too correct.*

History and reality are themselves inventing a kind of literature.

Xi Chuan stopped writing poetry for a time. Then he started writing (his word) "bad" poetry.

Donald Revell. He's absolutely correct. But maybe too correct.

What does he think we're building in the former wilderness of sky?

---

readability of forms. "Yes, indeed, I think the Ruin a great Addition to the Beauty of the Lake. There is something so vastly picturesque, and pleas-ing to the Imagination in such Objects, that they are a great Addition to every Landskip." **7** I think Miłosz loves the nail. **8** In his essay "Style

Amenable, tolerable, useful, pleasant, beautiful, ravaged, ruined.

We regard the land.

Comes as a Reward," Xi Chuan reports and comments on the catalogue
of poetic styles compiled by Sikong Tu (837-908).   **9** To write honestly
about your times: I don't know, is that even possible? In his introduction
to a selection of Xi Chuan's lyric and anti-lyric poems, Lucas Klein writes:

At Elliot Lake the lowland as if rendered
with a palette knife, sludge white lavished then scraped into

burnt spindles of tree in a ragged trough
flanked by igneous rock, a few yellowed spruce hanging on.

A grey bank rises, massive, and above it,
thinner, also grey: sky

or a farther hill, we don't know.
A few dark specks on the ridge

lean toward a box-like structure,
people, maybe, moving toward shelter.

Near the shelter, a thin blue line
angles sharply down the bank

and away. Back in the valley, the broken, abandoned valley,
three lengths of pipe materialize in the debris.

"Gaining recognition first as one of the post-Obscure poets in the late
eighties, his writing was defined by a condensed lyricism in the Western
modernist mode. Today, he writes expansive prose-poems that meditate
on awkwardness and paradox at the individual and international levels

On my way to town I pass a small lake where often in summer I see a small boat at anchor, drifting lazily around its mooring, someone from the campground out fishing.

On the north side a high cliff of metamorphic rock juts, forcing a bend in the road.

Heading east the lake opens a vista on my right — mist hanging, or blue ripples, or bright pixels of sunlight; heading west, the dark rock looms. I've seen bald eagles on this stretch, and storms gathering, and every kind of light.

What is the difference between knowledge and memory?

Heading home with the car full of groceries it's along this stretch I'll remember what I forgot, just past the place where brush is growing up through the foundations of an abandoned building.

I feel happy when I remember I've forgotten broccoli.

I'm not so sure about the events of my life. Do I really want to remember them?

Susan Sontag thinks maybe not. *To make peace is to forget.*

My old friend says he doesn't remember the thing I'm finally apologizing for.

It's meant as a form of kindness.

But it makes me furious.

---

simultaneously. The main shift came in 1989 — the year not only of the students' democracy and workers' rights demonstrations, crushed June 4th in Tian'anmen Square, but also of the death of two of Xi Chuan's closest writer-friends, Hai Zi and Luo Yihe (the former at his own hand)—

13

The only thing I remember about Professor Marcos Dragoumis's 1997 lecture in a small airy library in Athens on the folk music of Crete

apart from the scratchy sound of the recordings collected in the field in the 1920s,

and being there with Sallie Latch who this very minute is on her way to Samos to help the Greek people with the Syrian refugees,

and meeting Eric Davis who played horn — Sallie thought he had a crush on me — it didn't last long — nevertheless I learned a few things about philosophy — not to mention language —

is an aside —

In the aside, Professor Dragoumis, noticeably exercised, said anyone who claims the folk music of Greece has nothing in common with the folk music of Turkey, *well, that's just nationalism — and not the good kind!*

I could use a bit more of that old scratchy sound.

I don't know where Eric Davis is now, whether he's still alive or still plays horn — or both —

after which Xi Chuan stopped writing almost completely for three years. When he re-emerged, his form had changed: he was writing a poetry of the anti-lyric, a poetics of contradiction that deconstructed the aestheticism and musicality of his previous self... Later, he would describe his

Xi Chuan says to write honestly of your times means being loyal to your sense of reality.

Loyal, as in scraping your sense of reality to the bone.

---

focus on the paradox, or oxymoron, as one poetic reaction to China's political and economic realities." **10** John Dixon Hunt, on how we assess land. Try these words on other things. On, say, women's bodies. **11** Edward Burtynsky documented the impact of uranium mines in

15

An obelisk in a wood, a jar in Tennessee.

Hello large, unreachable, disturbing, dangerous, hostile, discomfiting, raw. Meet norm, custom, habit, manner, rule, order, law.

Hey, here's Jared on the tractor, come to cut the hay.

---

northern Ontario in large-scale chromogenic prints in the mid 1990s. I can't stop looking at *Uranium Tailings #12, Elliot Lake, Ontario.*   **12** Mist that swallows memory is a feature of Kazuo Ishiguro's *The Buried Giant,* a novel I couldn't put down. Post-Arthurian England is at a precarious

My obelisk is daily cooking.

No one will ever place a wreath at its foot or immortalize it in poetry or put a plaque on it.

No one stands before its polished face, reflecting.

An onion can be peeled right down to nothing.

---

peace thanks to the mist that allows neighbours and families to forget the conflicts, and even the relationships, that burden their past. **13** War, famine, poverty, greed, crime, punishment, adventure. Is there any part of the world that has not been altered by people displaced by

17

Mist over the river mirrored in the river.

Distant hills rising behind distant hills, blue resolving to pink in the dawn mist.

Everything curves away from the dam, even the island, barren except for equipment, the yellow shed, bright tarps, narrow road, power lines.

The dam's unfinished end gapes.

Cranes sit idle on its face and ridge.

It's the kind of scene you might find on paper money.

A minuscule barge crosses.

Upriver, in a house near the shore, a young Du Fu dreaming of dolphins wakes to the distant steady pounding, high in the hills, of machines dismantling a village.

one or more of these? The 1923 population exchange between Greece and Turkey uprooted 1.6 million people. As of 2017, some 4.8 million Syrian people were homeless, in transit, displaced across the borders of their country. What does that music sound like? What will it sound like in 100 years?

The house, located in pastoral farmland, disappeared into the sinkhole's gaping maw.

A neighbour heard a strange groan and drove toward the source.

He stood at the precipice and stared into the abyss, into *a different kind of blackness*, an amphitheatre of darkness.

He could see the house, tilted precariously. The garage was shorn off. A cellphone was ringing.

The river was high. It seeped into the clay underlying it.

The clay turned to liquid and flowed downhill.

The earth cracked and shifted, earth cracked and shifted, earth cracked and shifted, slabs of solid ground thrust up like a row of dominoes.

A man driving a red truck, humming along to oldies on the radio, drove straight into the hole. It took him an hour to climb out.

The trees were gone, the earth was gone, it was the end of the world.

The people were found very close to one another in the family room in the basement, where they'd been watching hockey on TV.

---

14 What Xi Chuan actually says: "To be honest to oneself means to be loyal to your sense of reality. You don't need to mirror that reality, but you need to be symmetrical to the vigor of history and of reality. Style comes as a reward. And now, I can say that I don't care about it." I think

As I was writing this, four deer crossed the field. First an adult emerged from the woods. She stopped when she saw the cat on the porch, who had himself just emerged from the house. The doe spread her ears wide, alert. A fawn came, then another, bounding out of the woods. The doe herded them close and they crossed the field steadily, unhurried, the doe looking over at the porch every so often. A third fawn, very small, sprang out and caught up with the others just as they were vanishing into woods on the other side.

The field is bare again, but the stubble in it is thicker. The woods that border it have spread open. I can see every stump, every sapling, every fallen limb. Everything's brightened. Everything's more of itself.

Xi Chuan is writing with a nail in his shoe. In the good sense.   **15** And I'm still lying around in the hammock …   **16** Transformation of the raw: the pathways my ingredients have travelled, the indignities they've suffered! The first book that taught me to cook was Paula Wolfert's

I buried the scarlet tanager that crashed into the window.

I'd never seen such a perfect bright red, red that flooded my skull, throat, lungs.

Its head lolled softly to the side when I lifted it. Ants were crawling in its eyes, taking it back.

Red that raced through me, erasing everything that wasn't red, *maybe it wasn't the thump I'd heard earlier, maybe it just happened, maybe it wasn't too late.*

A tuft of feathers stuck to the glass.

I buried the scarlet tanager that crashed into my window. I shovelled earth into the hole. I covered it. I leaned on the shovel. I crouched, I laid my hand on the mound, I said this, I had nothing to say.

World of Food (later renamed, aptly, *Mostly Mediterranean*).   **17** In the first poem of the sequence "Autumn Meditations," written in 766, Du Fu, by then elderly, notes the pounding of washing blocks in a village high in the mountains as preparations are made for winter. Edward Burtynsky's

In this life we walk on the roof of hell, gazing at flowers.

Walking the flattened grass, are we walking the deer's path or are they walking ours?

Geese low overhead en route to Willow Pond — what's a house to them?

---

photograph "Dam #2" depicts China's Three Gorges Dam in two visual languages, one that recalls traditional Japanese woodblock prints, the other early 20th century futuristic illustrations of marvels of engineering. See also Robert Hass, "Ezra Pound's Proposition," concerning economic

Large rectangles of light sweep across the hayfield.

The wind is high — the hay itself is not moving, only the light on the hay.

Only the clouds and the utmost branches.

And then the wind spirals down, down, a shadow crosses, the hay bends down.

Yes, I would like to be a poet of the world,

of train wrecks, oils spills, ravaged lands, desecrated bodies, whole languages forbidden and excised,

of the demented and the near extinct, of extraction, transgression,

of the canyon after a landslide, the flooded urban plain,

a circle of people bigger than a pipeline, tent camps with tanks of clean water, rebuilt rooms of a burned-out town,

ululatory.

Wouldn't the images show us holding hands?

Wouldn't the light already be fading from green to murk?

---

and environmental impacts of Thailand's Pak Mun Dam. **18** *In memoriam* Richard Prefontaine, Lyne Charbonneau, Anaïs Prefontaine, and Amélie Prefontaine. **19** A well-used narrow path crosses this pleasing vista, but I'm not always lucky enough to be looking when the animals appear.

23

And every now and then, I don't know how, maybe a whole lot of sense impressions fire at once, the modes of perception snap, and everything slows.

Like Whitman, *I think I will do nothing for a long time …*

---

20 How many scarlet tanagers have I seen in nearly a decade in this place? Exactly one. That one.   21 Some versions of Issa's poem in English put a capital H on "hell."   22 My newsfeed is filled with images of ruin, images that flicker and fade but never really go away. I click through a story,

Pools of spilled slag, rivers of it, orange and gleaming.

The grain of rusted hulls in ship-breaking yards, sharp against humid skin.

Hot waste, e-waste, tweezers and bare hands picking through it, steam.

Pixel boards of pink uniforms opening onto pixel boards of pink uniforms.

Black sand hills stretching across the steel yards to the horizon.

Beauty come forward through a cloud of gas, the alchemy of imagery, chemical, digital, chimerical, romancing the apocalypse —

Cypresses at dawn, and the bluish air in the valleys

writing the rhythm of the next stories I'll see. I click on random stories to confuse the future story. This is not a form of witness.   **23** As Alden Nowlan says, "How long have I lain here? / Well, it is still summer. But is it the same / summer I came? I must remember / not to ask myself questions..."

How far off   those fields
those evenings   mine and not mine
         cicadas   in ruins

the play of light that does and does not resemble a searchlight

---

24 And so we arrive at the lyric-anti-lyric (and back at "In Milan"): I can, therefore I don't. Burtynsky catalogues destruction and production. Are we looking at beauty or horror? The photographs don't tell us what to feel. See also Louis Helbig's lyric, painterly photographs of the Athabasca tar

Brazil, Serra Pelada.
A trough in the earth
crawling with beetles.

Coiled tentacles
fossilized in stone.

Bronzed men
caught mid-stride
scaling the pit walls,

spoils fused to their backs.

Salgado, their armour
is burnt on —

What am I looking at?

sands collected in *Beautiful Destruction*.　**25** The danger now is writing
poems about ruins as though ruins were cicadas. See also Goya, *Los
Caprichos*.　**26** The Brazilian photographer Sebastião Salgado documented
a wide range of human experience, from nearly incomprehensible acts of

We're standing on steel bleachers, alone except for a crow. It's the weekend, no one is working.

We've walked a long way uphill from a locked gate. Tire tracks and a trail of blood on the road — hunters have been here.

The pit spreads out in a wide crescent, a white sea, a drained sea, a gash, a crater, a moonscape with roads and stationary machines like toys, a carved marble stage set for a play.

Looking at it is like looking at a town in a valley from a descending jet.

Looking at ourselves on the descent.

---

human desire to nearly unbearable images of suffering. On the gold mines of Brazil, Salgado writes: "Every time a section finds gold, the men who carry up the loads of mud and earth have, by law, the right to pick one of the sacks they brought out. And inside they may find fortune and freedom.

The first house had no eaves.

Then houses began to have porches, where it became pleasant to take a warm or cool drink of an evening.

Dappled light on the walls seemed a reflection of the time before houses, the forest waving its leaves, beauty and shelter among its many gifts.

The light shifts.

I refill my glass and watch the watery leaf-shapes swim on the cedar planks.

What do I know of the time before houses?

It gets in the nose, cedar does, hangs on the heels of a warm day with the frisson of crickets and occasional bull-frog blurt, and still — the sun low over the knoll now — light wavers in the eaves

A crow calls.

In a few minutes I'll get up and go in and light the stove. It might be the first fire in a pit in the first house but for the door, and everything else that came after.

The sun sets.

Here on the porch, the breeze picks up. Shadows close. The small sounds of breathing.

So their lives are a delirious sequence of climbs down into the vast hold and climbs out to the edge of the mine, bearing a sack of earth and the hope of gold." Many of his photographs are almost impossible to look at.
27 The Tatlock quarry in the Lanark Highlands occupies a huge swath of

During our lives, time unfolds, unfolds, unfolds. And then it ends — for us, anyway.

It's complicated: the world unfolds to enfold us.

---

land where white marble is extracted and trucked 47 km to the Omya plant for further processing. Two sets of bleachers close to a chain link fence invite spectators to watch operations in the marble quarry's main pit, far away from administrative buildings, weigh scales, loading rigs and trucks.

When the bear came, I was searching for blackberries near the quarry.

I had already walked through a wet hollow where wild mint grew, and gathered some.

I was carrying the mint in my pocket, pinching it and sniffing its oil on my fingers, when the movement came, a dark fleck drifting down the side of my vision.

The bear did not notice me till I stepped back, brambles grazing my arms and face.

A shadow moved in and settled, enclosing us, a shadow with an odour like mineral ash.

I don't know why but I held out the bunch of mint, held it straight out from my chest at arm's length, held it still, nothing but brambles supporting me.

The bear studied me, then grunted and turned over a rock, swatted the ground she'd opened, and moved off into the woods, which folded around her.

MORNING LIGHT

Without mention of blossoms
Miłosz gets the tree in the poem from translucent to laden with fruit.
Years passed, not days, while he slept,
and that tree must have flowered many times.

In the same way, we turn over mid-dream
or after love, those beautiful hours
we know were passed in the company of genius
but have forgotten in the particulars.

We know the tree stands for promise
and for the desire, which comes much later, for atonement.
We stand at the west-facing window
and let the buildings opposite turn gold, then back to brick.

SALAMANDER

Around here most cattle farms have gone the way of the railroad.

I drive along Hwy 7 toward town past many beauties, some natural, some ramshackle, including a boarded-up former motel and restaurant I would have found convenient.

Sometimes I fantasize about taking over the lease and re-opening it as A Really Happening Joint.

That idea lasts till about the next bend in the road.

Across the highway from the motel, Silver Lake shimmers like a cocktail at noon, like the weekend you're about to spend with your lover.

I come to the point thick with pine trees and whizz on by.

Often just before I get to the point I notice two deeply suntanned men sitting on a floating dock below the highway.

Further along there's a shady pasture that rises up on the lake side where the road turns away, cows in it that might be shadows or boulders.

I have to be careful on this corner because in a way I'm driving not just through space but also through time, and hey, I'm driving a ghost car through a theme-park panorama.

On the way back after a refreshing fill-up at Bob's Petrocan and a quick duck into the Freshmart the lake is on my left, and on my right the real rolling fields open up, grand, dotted with hay bales and looking very modern.

Some of the lakeside campsites at Silver Lake are so close to the road I can just about read the tent labels.

Once out on a walk I watched a salamander cross the road.

Salamanders have a distinctive way of moving that's often compared to licking flames.

The left back foot darts forward, then the left front, then in a little bursting twitch the right back foot darts, then the right front, and so on.

If I don't write all this down it will eat me up.

Just like that little flame licking across the road, mid-morning it was, and the sky darkened.

I couldn't see anything else for a good while after; it gushed rain, then a bittern flew up from the marsh.

FIELDWORK

Overnight soft hollows appeared in the field
and a narrow path to the edge of the small wood.

Animals bedding down, travelling somewhere, or wind.
My dream of gravity, carried off by mosquitoes.

No gesture is unreadable.
Slipping on my mouse-brown felt shoes

I wish the plane the rebels shot down
could have hung on an updraft

the way a piece of field fluff hangs on a current of air,
suspended as though in a web,

not blown apart but held.
We go through life forgetting

how tender things can be.
That timothy scent and a pinch of nearly invisible seeds

slip inside me and prick my bronchioles.
Where is my father now, and the little burble

he breathed through in his chest?
He'd been on the blood machine, which cleaned him

while he watched *Dragons' Den* or slept.
Su-Lin clamped his arm in two places when he was done

and twisted the tube awkwardly from the fistula.
That vein had burst and been repaired at least once.

He fixed on the screen against the pain
and turned his gaze to me when he could smile.

I leaned into his shoulder and inhaled.
Then he sobbed, and stupidly I said,

Don't be sad, don't be sad, hating
what I was saying. — *Such a wind across the meadow,*

I should have said. *The felled hay in curved rows.*
My father, who'd held me like a sparrow to his chest.

The sunlight here lances, though the swooshing of trees
is thoroughly refreshing. Everything

seems fine with the world though terrible things happen.
Wind rustles the highest boughs like a cat

pawing through a box of tissue paper, travels
the room cooling my legs, nudges

the tabs of my hoodie so they jingle lightly.
White cigar clouds painted onto the sky.

A large bird soars, drifts down on a draft.
Su-Lin's blue-gloved hands.

The sky's the same, the canal the same, the streets same, the crane.
The ditches, yards, fences, doors, the gravel road, the shore.

The blue hull, sails, the bed, the narrow corridor.
All gestures are unreadable.

The field meets the grove in a borderland of thorns.
I can't bring myself to do anything.

WAR & PEACE

The old prince, his father, is in serious decline.
Bald Hills, that beloved dream, in enemy hands.
These thoughts rise in a cloud
with the dust in the road along which he leads his regiment

and like the dust, once stirred, never quite settle,
only waft, collecting in swirls at the men's backs,
clinging to their shabby uniforms,
flecking their beards and hair, sifting into eyes, ears, skin ...

They march away from Smolensk, which is lost.
In each man's face — whether brutish, resigned, lost,
devoted, deceitful, careless, roguish, afraid,
empty, or about to erupt — in each arrangement of eyes

the prince sees the same thing: himself,
and his dream of himself. *If only*
it would rain — They march away from battle
toward battle, leaving dust in their wake.

DRIFT

Tracks in the snow, hardened overnight to shattering: cat, wild turkeys, us circling the house. New snow collecting in their centres.

Out to the screen house for sunrise viewing and back, coffee steaming.

Each time the Chihuly glass balls come up on my screen saver, I ask myself: what if I'd never left the coast? Would I still be wearing those old deerhide slippers?

The pull of backwash in pebbles at the tide line, *line* a gesture towards.

When I said *the sound of pebbles in the backwash settles something in me*, the person I said it to flowered a little, as though I'd said something absolute.

The bee slips into the rose whether I'm watching or not. That's what summer is.

That's what summer is, everything getting on with becoming more of itself before it dies. Don't we ever tire of it? Ever?

A long hair left in the bowl of the sink. A crescent moon.

Crossing the prairie by train in winter under a full moon, moving east toward a new life in an unknown city, everything I would need I could see from the moving window.

Lights of the next town on the horizon. Beyond them, another horizon.

I say my name and drop a penny into the lily pond. Dragonflies settle and lift, settle and lift, seedpods on a summer breeze.

It's how we all got here, drift. Soon there won't be a trace.

When the snow melted in the thaw between storms I went looking for chives at the edge of the herb bed and found the heart of an old wasps' nest fallen from an eave.

Ingenious device, this paper house. The wind rushes in its cells.

FORGIVE ME, I THOUGHT IT WAS
JUST WIND IN THE MARSH REEDS

I am seventeen and about to disappear forever.
I don't even know what santolina is.

I've never seen an alabaster temple in a field of grain,
moonlight like combed hair.

Facing the sun I find more shadow than light,
trees using light to become invisible.

That thing we never think of
courses under everything—

rain keeps coming back—
that's why bagpipes were invented.

Will the Dragons put much stock in bullfrog futures
once the sites and even the tools of extraction are used up?

Excising what isn't "useful" isn't useful.

The map we bring with us isn't useful,
and the rest is work.

A pine cone drops to the ground.

Those men in the ring like dogs, did they choose that?
Do they dream of picnics stretching long into evening?

LOST & FOUND

The checkout clerk was a certain age, and very blond. The packer was young, his eyes like sponges. Taking everything in, looking everywhere but in the bags he was packing.

He was packing the bags by feel, fixed on something else, quick, not fumbling exactly but undistinguished by grace.

Grace would have been a good name for the cashier, who was large of voice and gesture, shapely, and vocally very happy; she was proud, effusive, made great claims of love for everyone at work, her *family of work*.

I was reminded of Voula, who ran the Sunset Bar on the highest street in town on an island I stayed on for awhile.

She sat with me at a table once to answer a question.

I'd spent the day walking: along the Roman road bordered by pines to an inland hill town where everything was closed so I continued down to the western coast through pines and cypress and overgrown fields and kicked around in the edges of waves getting doused and pliable.

The walk back through the pine forest restored me.

I was stopped by a line of mourners threading up from the edge of town to the church in the central square.

I wanted to watch but not to seem to, so slanted my watching downward.

One of the crones stepped aside and approached me, closed her hand over mine, pressing a packet of Sesame Snaps into my palm, staring straight into my eyes — I'd never been so seen.

When the procession had passed I walked on, refreshed myself at the tavern where men were setting up for the funeral feast, not open really but willing to sell me a beer.

Then I retraced the ancient way back to where I was staying.

After a nap in which I dreamed of nothing I wandered out to the Sunset Bar and asked Voula my question, *Why she did gave, me a stranger?*

I could see Voula searching the words. Her face grew clear and intent, she looked away and looked back and then opened her arms slightly and flattened her palms, the burning end of her cigarette brushing the blue table top, and she pinched up her shoulders — there's a lexicon of shrugs in some languages —

She found the words in the shrug and spoke them like it was not a foreign language to her, *Because, you, are people!*

This is the way Grace at the checkout on the last day of November told me about her job.

And at the end, after the flurry of declining free delivery and donating the free roll of holiday wrapping paper to the community center collection box, I'd lost track of my gloves, and in pawing through my bags I found a bunch of bananas that belonged to the guy ahead of me.

Fortunately, he had accepted the free delivery so Grace dispatched the young packer to add them back to his box.

Out in the car repacking my bags I found two English cucumbers, a kilo of tomatoes and a box of 3.25% milk I didn't recognize so I took those back inside.

This time the young packer's eyes swam uncertainly as Grace's ebullience changed shade, from what I'd call sparkling to something more like just sparks.

And I remembered suddenly I'd meant to buy milk and had forgotten so tried to make a joke of how it was a good thing for me.

But we were both a little awkward, the packer and me, me in seeing his mistake and he in being seen, and Grace sent him off somewhere, scolding him like you might a dog, and went back to pulling people through her line, and I went off and got my milk and when I went back through her line it took her a minute to remember me, and maybe she didn't really, I mean, who could remember every person that passed through her line on a busy morning?

But maybe she did, and anyway we shared a laugh and the same young man handed over my bag with the same shy smile.

It's what we all want, isn't it?

A crackly crust, good solid structure underneath, chewy and marvellous.

BRIDGE

I approach the bridge I've never been on.
The pale span hangs from steel wires
pinning a fold of sky to the sky.

Although the river, thickened with islands, does not resemble
the bays and harbours I sailed with my young father,
it's still a blue mirror far below as I cross.

The headlights and windscreen of a transport truck
rise toward me in the adjacent lane like a messenger
carrying unknown cargo to the places I've left.

And so I press on.
At the tollbooth I hand over bills, receive coins in return.
Our hands don't touch in the exchange

though a strand of fine hair clings, sailing straight out
on a draft before letting go.

THE BEAUTY OF THE TABLE

For we are all so mortal that we hardly live.
— Czesław Miłosz

He stands up, slightly drunk, looks at the sea.
Like Prospero, he feels everything to be in his power.
But it isn't a storm he's after, he's just going for a piss.

As he bumps against the table, everything beautifies:
the knives, the plates, the old wooden table itself,

even the ache in his thigh where he knocked it,
the sea, the beautiful tipsiness, all wobble and resolve,
even approaching death, which he can almost see

surfing in on the waves in its dark wetsuit —
okay, not quite that.

He swabs the dribble at the end of the flow.
Not death, then. But to know it's coming,
to know what we share will continue being shared,

that boundary is beautiful.
And the next drink, and the splendid sea, lapping the legs of our table.

CRUISE

Blue again. A little darker today, and more rippled, I think, but it's easy to lose track. I punch my pillow, even though the room attendants will tidy everything while we're at brunch, boring ourselves blind with iterations.

Riveted to the wall above the bed, a portrait of our ship on the occasion of her launch decades ago. Bouquets the size of my mother's house. Champagne in fountains. Outfits like the plumage of tropical birds. Not a child in sight, though that doesn't mean, of course, there weren't any.

Where in the world do we come from? We drift around — oh, we do, call it what you will. Navigating the navigable, ignoring the rest, except when we glimpse over a rail on our way again to the dining room, on the horizon or through a rift in the blue curtain, a quickness, shining, like something we recall we'd been meaning to do.

SO I BEG YOU, NO MORE OF THOSE LAMENTATIONS

We used to read in old poets about the scent of the earth —
Now I walk through rooms holding my cup of coffee
looking into the shadowed streets without seeing

until a bright puddle arrests me like a doe in a clearing,
absolutely still, expanding in its brightness
as the sun crosses the parking lot, slowly,

and one by one particulars assemble: grit,
muck, rubbish, dirty cars, concrete curb, the red brick wall and darker bricks
among them, twelve orange tabs on the power lines at the corner,

juncture points on the pole and on the wires themselves, the pole
grey as a dove's breast, a red slash through a black truck on a white sign,
a sky-blue poster like a hole in the wall

the beautiful doe, releasing my gaze, bounds through.

SHIFT IN THE WEATHER

cloud breaking up —
it's there forever, that yellow crane
in my mind's eye

packing again
before I finish unpacking

violets spring up
everywhere, even where
we didn't plant them

we've been married
a long time!

a thicket of brambles
half obscures the rock pile
wild onions cover the rest

none of the olive pits
have sprouted yet in the lawn

I would dearly love to be forgiven
my foolish ways
too, Miłosz

whatever they are
or might become

MY DUENDE

each time I ride the escalator with my duende
a little voice in my ear
says I should walk

oh shut up, I say
and grip my duende's hand a little tighter

every second cell of marram grass
under a microscope
is a happy face — well, no wonder!

voices leap out
as someone opens a door

suddenly all the clocks are wrong
everything that binds me to my life is wrong
and I'm late for breakfast again

everything's so bright
we never see it anymore

we, that is to say I,
the multiplicity that is I,
the compound I,

don't, that is to say
action! cut! go back

ROOMS, AND NOT JUST INTERIORS

morning is when I miss you most
and afternoon and evening
while awake and while asleep I miss you

apparition disparue
light spilling through rain clouds

and summer drew to a close
and I travelled
and returned to school

what is my life, after all?
and where did I put it?

ODE

These cold blue dusky mornings, softly cloudy up high, the comfortable rolling of tires on pavement like sighs, the crane on the St. Patrick building site quiet, underlit by a harsh industrial light.

Across the rooftops, lights over the freeway like a small village.

Everything's bare but for the yellow shrubs overhanging the low wooden fence between the parking lots. Sidewalks and gutters are papered with a mash of leaves.

The dawn sky darkens toward winter, closes in on the busy glare, closes it up inside a spun shell like a wasps' nest.

At 6:30 precisely the crane swings around through all the compass points, comes to settle pointing west.

How I would like to find that panel in my heart that opens, and open it.

*

What's that gentle tapping below the shush of tires, as though at great distance?

       That's Vlad with his hammer, building the concrete forms.

What's that small vibration grinding in my bones?

       That's the truck hauling girders slowing down outside your window.

What's that hot musk like a skunk in a corner?

       That's what they dug up when they first broke ground.

What's that tang behind my teeth after coffee?

       That's the yellow crane swinging back and forth above the maple crowns.

What's that form racing toward me in the sky, looking so much like a cloud?

       That's a cloud, a dark cloud, just as it seems. Look how it glows, violet and gold, like the inside of the quietest room.

*

Behind and above the yellow crane
the sky is an almost uniform grey
streaked with lighter bits,
messy and thick like putty.

Not a cloud I'd want to lose my head in.

The longer I look, though, the more it seems
that cloud is all that's in my head

and the crane's yellow arm
is what I lean on when I lean
into the place that had just been view.

*

A large room where a lot of people were having casual sex, not hot really, just sort of nice, before the earthquake and the building falling in.

Waking to the whole building shaking and the fear of it really happening, an earthquake or the building falling in. People in the building across the street grabbing things and dashing outside in underwear.

I hunkered in a corner. No one knew what to do.

Waking from that to nothing, no panicky people, just morning light catching the yellow crane three blocks away and a kind of helpless relief.

The crane is pivoting. When it stops and points east, it looks like it's pointing up toward the sun. As it swings south the angle seems to change, though once it passes it's clear from where I lie that it's on the level.

Hurrying past the building site I find the wrong glasses in my case, turn to say something friendly to someone who's not my friend, who hurries past me toward a young woman who is waiting, clearly in love. An octopus swims through the unfinished rooms, bruised purplish tentacles emerging from the window holes.

The life of the imagination — would you choose it over the life of the mind?

What would you do, waking to the dawn sky in the mirror brighter than the same sky outside?

*

As though winter had permeated these objects,

morning light and the coming storm animating,
galvanizing them,

the crane's short arm, the counterweight hanging from it,
vigorous,

each ready for its action to begin, light

sliding along the yellow steel, pinging off every bolt and join,
blistering, magnifying

the flat grey weight that holds everything steady
like a great square moon

maintaining a distance, always the same distance,
light

bouncing into the filigree of leafless trees, dropping,
dropping, brightening

as it drops so I forget the storm
gathering there.

In the mirror across from my window
a man moves down a set of porch stairs in shadow,

small, awkward,
a rogue villager lifted from a Renaissance tableau.

One hand slides along the rail as he descends.
The other drags a dark swollen bag,
a bouquet in reverse,

the sky white,
the storm imminent.

*

They rest lightly on the invisible floor, these clouds
glowing with inner buoyancy, grey and glowing with immanence.

All the greys on the grey-scale lolling, lightly resting
their porpoise bodies, their eel-selves, weed-strands, bobbling ocean
junk.

If all the souls lost at sea this decade stood on each other's shoulders —
the tycoons, troops, tourists, students, sailors, politicians, pirates,
pilots, pets, honeymooners, flight attendants, fishermen, drunkards,
divers, criminals, citizens, children —

they'd reach the bellies of these clouds, so the one on top
could strike them. Such pearls would spill out! Bright confetti

of lives and portions of lives yet to live would spill down
smothering everything with unspeakable richness.

Instead the world is covered in snow, which returns to the sky
only to fall again, though I beg for plum blossoms

and would settle for feathers. The sky
is thumping us on the head like a stern teacher

from an old book no one reads anymore, shouting,
Fools! Have you learned nothing?

*

Watching the yellow crane, thinking about the book I've been reading, excited and unsure, opened by it.

The narrator meets a lovely girl. He says he wishes she could grow up quickly, grow into a girlfriend for his old age.

I set the book down.

The crane revolves. No: the jib swivels.

I feel the need to walk a little.

*

The temperature drop is hard on the new foundation plants.

They dwindle and show more stem than the same specimens further down the row.

Look how that rugosa rose throws up hips at dogs and walkers! Sun-warmed as any summer berry, in spite of frost.

Their dry little brown crowns are pointed yet modest. *Oh, weren't we all flowers once?* they intimate; *bees knew us, your nose knew us, summer breezes too.*

We still hold secrets in our gleaming hearts —

What am I saying? Plants don't speak English.

And they certainly have no interest in me.

How still they are against the concrete wall, the old ones flush, the young ones thin and almost beaten.

*

I go for a walk, and when I get back, my house is reduced to cobweb.

Young oaks, hurry up and grow into a house for me!

*

Boom, traveller, plumb, hook, cab — I will miss the yellow crane when the building is finished.

The crane has just lifted a load of steel I-beams and lowered them to a point I can't see, though I can see the figures of people walking along the roof.

Days close in on a wasps' nest of days.

Is there a procedure for emptying myself?

As when the sky suddenly empties and resurges toward a storm.

*

I stretch out my back, de-kink like an insect unfolding.
Haul the blue bin down to the street, deposit it with the others
beside the tree.

It's full of empty things that were full before I emptied them.
It will be emptied into a truck full of empty things
which will be emptied into the crusher.

If there's a name for this
I'm sure I'll forget it.

*

Girl on a sidewalk heading towards the metro in rain
burgundy and nylon wetly tangled
across grit and chain-link
a dark scurry

lost-world receptor
many-pronged
instrument

more wind than song
more push than rain

*

What is so complicated about tenderness? The whole world is wounded.

I opened the curtains at 6:50 a.m. to a rich blue sky flocked with puffball clouds, airy yet firm, dreamy piglets of cloud, the yellow crane over the treetops catching the morning light, its long arm elegant, definitive, reaching northward.

Coffee, and the clatter of a scrap metal truck on the street.

If I am concrete and river, if a direction, which?

Desire, loneliness, wind in the flowering almond — surely these are the great, the inexhaustible subjects —

A thing is sliding along the crane. The arm swivels; now it is out of sight.

The world of dew is the world of dew. And yet, and yet —

Wash, dress, eat, drive, park, talk, perform, record, return, drive, eat, undress, wash, repeat. Note a few random beauties.

What is "really living," anyway?

Now that we really are.

*

Turning left onto the main road coming home, the gilded sky
deepening to indigo, there in a gap between buildings

the thin moon, long and keen, low in the sky as a street lamp,
an open *c* turned, stretched, a loose hair, a thread of zest.

To what summoned? And to whom? blindly driving somewhere
and it's holy, isn't it, Miłosz, to be called like that, drawn by force toward

the unattainable, small valley past *horizons of woolly haze.*
Then in an instant called from sleep, summoned through the interchange

of dreams. How like yawning,
pulling the curtains open on a fine morning

to cloud radiating up and out from some low point behind buildings,
cloud arms tinted pink as cake, holy spokes radiating out from the blind

wound of the railyards, Our Lady of industrial wrack, traffic squall.
Between the glass of my window and the brick, steel and concrete beyond,

panels of light and shadow tilting.
As I stood looking, two pale legs and part of an arm

floated forward in the dim interior across the street, the very clouds
come forward through the city and up the stairs.

And why not? Why not? Why should our bodies not appear
as transient forms? Smoke and nothing, gathered in a moistness.

Apparition with Blue Coffee Mug

Apparition in a Window

Suppose I pass this woman every day on the street and don't know her?

*

When form changes, meaning changes, but my father's gaze
is my father's gaze

whether I'm beside him with my hand on his good arm
or just looking at him in a photograph

or catching his grin in the last few leaves of the maple
flashing and waving — *summoned* is a mild word for it.

I reach up to the curtains
and if I'm not careful I'll pull the whole contraption down.

*

What's that tearing I hear in the distance?
>That's Vlad, ripping away the forms.

What's that tremor I feel in my ribs?
>That's the jackhammer, ripping away the street.

What's that hot wave like gas at the pump?
>That's the future, spilling over the river.

What's that thickness gathering under my tongue?
>That's the sludge of knowledge and memory, festering in
>the canal.

What's that rushing at me from all directions?
>That's your life, disguised as traffic. Look how it gathers
>in morning light like molten glass.

*

Slowly the canal is returning to life — the stink of algae expands, cyclists appear, dogs trot on leashes, sparrows flower the shrubs along the bank.

Then the gates are opened upstream and the fresh, still-chill water rushes out to meet its ride to the sea.

Half submerged, ballooning, a plastic bag snagged on concrete billows like a sail.

A rust-coloured sail dragged in the furrow of a wave ...

*

Evening began to turn everything golden.
My city, though ugly, broken down, grit-whipped, stricken

is also vibrant, shrill in the way summer insects
are shrill, calling out for their lives

and once I pushed through the uglier elements of hatred and fear
I could hear more birds.

As I approached, the skyline grew
bright in front of distant hills, and in front of the skyline

giant screens depicted pixelated towers
multiplexing the future.

Everything's so bright!

The people inside them weren't doing anything
I recognized.

A STORY

In town, people were unzipping their coats,
carrying knit hats. It was the kind of day

strangers step aside for each other readily,
bestowing small gestures, the shoulder pull,
the bent arm aside, the chin tuck, the almost nod.

I cruised the block and parked in the last spot
behind an idling truck. It was the shady side, and I found it

a different world when I got out and began to walk,
a world of clutched fabric and flapping ends,
rough winds roiling up among buildings.

A phrase from an old song came to me
about walking on the sunny side of the street,

meant, I knew, as a lesson about complaining.
Such simplification is a hallmark of moral lessons.

Can it ever be otherwise?
Learning happens in retrospect, except in those most

charged and fortunate circumstances
when it drops on us like clear northern light.
The day before, I had walked the back field

through gem fires bursting from snow.
This, I thought, this is my beating heart.

Nothing had ever been more exciting or exact.
The world had opened, revealed its inner minerals.

I had no sense of having left my body
the way sometimes I have felt beside myself,
felt left,

yet my body, too, could have been flaring out,
maybe was.

Was it a vision of the end?
I came indoors, made coffee, went to my study as usual.

Each time I spoke of it reduced it a little
while expanding it in my mind.

This is how we reach knowledge of others:
finding what we cannot make understood.

Did we share a smile as we approached the door,
you and I?

The story lies; all stories lie;
they are like snow,

bodies formed by solidification of elements
with regular repeating structures of atoms and faces.
Most of the time they are all we have,

selves we reach out to
or hurry past, depending.

NOTES & ACKNOWLEDGEMENTS

The opening epigraph is from Czesław Miłosz's poem "In Milan."

"Obelisk" evolved from readings and misreadings in art and nature, some deliberate, some accidental. Thanks and apologies to:

Walter Benjamin, *Theses on the Philosophy of History*
Edward Burtynsky, *Uranium Tailings #12, Elliot Lake, Ontario* and *Dam #3* (large-scale chromogenic prints)
Du Fu, "Autumn Meditations"
William Gilpin, *A Dialogue upon the Gardens of the Right Honourable the Lord Viscount Cobham at Stow in Buckinghamshire*
John Dixon Hunt, *Gardens and the Picturesque*
Stuart Jeffries, "*Walter Benjamin: A Critical Life* review — gambler, womanizer, thinker" (*The Guardian*, 7 August 2014)
Kobayashi Issa in Robert Hass, *The Essential Haiku*
Lucas Klein, "Xi Chuan: Poetry of the Anti-Lyric" (*Cerise Press*, Summer 2011)
Don McKay, "Otherwise than Place" (*Deactivated West 100*)
Czesław Miłosz, "In Milan" (*The Collected Poems*)
Donald Revell, *The Art of Attention*
Sebastião Salgado, *Serra Pelada Gold Mine* (photographs)
Susan Sontag, *Regarding the Pain of Others*
Wallace Stevens, "Anecdote of the Jar"
Mary Vallis, "Mourning begins for Quebec family…" (*National Post*, 13 May 2010)
Wim Wenders and Julian Salgado, *The Salt of the Earth* (film)
Walt Whitman, "Song of Myself" (*Leaves of Grass*)
Virginia Woolf, *Three Guineas*
Xi Chuan. *Notes on the Mosquito: Selected Poems*, transl. Lucas Klein
Xi Chuan, "Style comes as a reward" (*almost island*, winter 2012)

Present in the interstices are Naz Arabaghian, Basho, Stephanie Bolster, Suzanne Buffam, Mary di Michele, Carolyn Forché, Louise Glück, Louis Helbig, Judith Herz, Kazuo Ishiguro, Nyla Matuk, John Miller, Valerie Murray, Alden Nowlan, Mary Ruefle, Gjertrud Schnackenberg, John Steffler, Wisława Szymborska, and Paula Wolfert among others; Andrew Ray's thoughtful blog *Some Landscapes* was a site of frequent return while I wrote.

Deep bow to Andrew Steeves and Gary Dunfield of Gaspereau Press who wrestled an earlier version of this poem into the pamphlet *Obelisk*, #33 in the Devil's Whim series.

"Morning Light" responds to Czesław Miłosz's "Window." The title and first line of "*So I beg you, no more of those lamentations*" are quoted from Miłosz's "Three Talks on Civilization." The epigraph to "The Beauty of the Table" is from Miłosz's poem "Table II."

Earlier versions of "Shift in the Weather," "My Duende," and "Rooms, and Not Just Interiors" were published in a limited-edition letterpress chapbook, *The Sky These Days* (Thee Hellbox Press, 2015). Grateful thanks to printer and publisher extraordinaire Hugh Barclay.

The section of "Ode" beginning "What is so complicated about tenderness?" includes lines from Louise Glück's "Summer Night" and from Issa. The section that begins "Turning left onto the main road coming home" quotes passages of Miłosz's "On the Road." The section that begins "Slowly the canal is returning to life" borrows from Miłosz's "From the Chronicles of the Town of Pornic (Our Lady of Recovery)." Thanks to Douglas Glover for publishing this poem under the title "Yellow Crane" in the journal *Numéro Cinq*.

Versions of some of these poems, sometimes under different titles, appeared in *Prism International, The Fiddlehead, Arc Poetry Magazine, The Malahat Review,* and *Vallum*. Thanks to the editors of these publications.

For the gifts of her remarkably attuned listening, generous editorial insight, and gentle nudging around some of my blind spots, my amazed and sincere thanks to Alayna Munce. Gratitude also to Kitty Lewis, Barry Dempster, Maureen Scott Harris, David Seymour, and the crack team at Brick Books, and to Natalie Olsen, who made the book beautiful.

Grants from the *Conseil des arts et des lettres du Québec* and the Canada Council made the writing of this book possible. I am grateful to those organizations for their continuing work in support of artistic creation.

Thanks also to John Abbott College and my colleagues and students in the English Department for support and encouragement.

Heartfelt thanks to Yoko's Dogs, the Pointe Sisters, Stephanie Bolster, Mary di Michele, and Sue Goyette.

To my dear companion John Steffler, this book is for you.

SUSAN GILLIS is a Montreal-based poet, teacher, and editor who has also lived on the Atlantic and Pacific coasts of Canada. A member of the collective Yoko's Dogs, she is the author of *Swimming Among the Ruins* (Signature Editions, 2000), *Volta* (Signature Editions, 2002), which won the A.M. Klein Prize for Poetry, *The Rapids* (Brick Books, 2012), *Whisk* (with Yoko's Dogs, Pedlar Press, 2013), and several chapbooks with Gaspereau Press. Susan spends a lot of time in rural Ontario, near Perth, where she does most of her writing.